UNFINISHED

Unfinished

PAUL CHENEOUR

Redgoldmusic.com

Contents

Copyright vi
Dedication vii

UNFINISHED

About The Author 29

Copyright © 2023 by Paul Cheneour

All rights reserved. No part of this book may be reproduced in any manner whatsoever without written permission except in the case of brief quotations embodied in critical articles and reviews.

First Printing, 2023

To those on the
path

Unfinished

I
You
We
Us
They
Them
Imaginary figments
In transition
All unfinished

In active stillness
No one sees you moving
In the seen world
No one sees your intention
In the unseen world
Great changes are under way
We still talk too much
Open your heart
Play more music
Let gratitude
Fly in and out

Looking over his shoulder
Snail turned to frog
And hissed
Keep off the grass
Frog taking no notice
Leapt
Towards
Himself

This slender moment
Trickles like sand through open fingers
Thoughts clamour for attention
A sudden laugh
A faint smile
A dim recollection
A fleeting glimpse
Something is dancing in the shadows
Caught on a solitary
Puff of wind

Your gaze rests on me
Now I have your attention
Reason sat down beside me
And demanded I listen
Hearing this Logic crept in
And readied her tentacles for a sudden embrace
Indifference and Aloofness sat muttering
Doubt Depression and Sadness looked at each other
Through clouds of confusion
And shuffled down the corridor
Suddenly Gratitude arrived
And overwhelmed us with love
My gaze rests on you now

Pause for a moment
Be very still
Breathe in
Fill your lungs
Let the sun like rain
Flow through you
Open your feeling centre
There is only peace in this moment
This is fulfilment
Stop looking
And see

These words write themselves
Caught like butterflies
Pouring from an open mouth
Dissolving hidden wounds
What do these ears hear
What do these eyes see
What is known
All I want is
A drop of real truth

The Sentinel shoots a fiery look
And observes you quizzically
As you approach the door-sill
He says
Do you think
You can pass through here
Without making full payment

Reaching the pillars of wisdom
The gatekeeper asks
Why did you come here
Do you think this is the right place
To find enlightenment
How many more times
Must you come here
Stop your feverish thinking
Slowdown and be quiet

A wild Dervish
Cries out in anguish
There is too much to tell
Over here under the moon
Alone in this concrete forest
No one hears the sound of a tree falling
Except the Dervish

Sacred mountain path
Beckons an earnest traveller
There are delights beyond imagination
To be found
Turn the key
Unlock your inspiration
Begin your journey today
Do not wait another thousand years

Scented air
Softens your rage
Look for connections in
The fragrance of the unknown
That sweeps ever upwards
From perfumed gardens

Feet make imprints in the sand
Rest your burden on the rocks
Move forward leave no trace
Embrace a peaceful surrender
Now look back
And see your marks disappear
Wash away the you in your self

Why are you dressed in plum red robes
I hear you ask
I have been sitting on this pole for years
Meditating watching and looking
And yes I have been through the eye of a needle
There is more to this existence
Than we can imagine

A generous compassion
Will soften your temper
Cease your anger
Move inward
Towards your centre
Go beyond sadness and grief
Look for clarity
Be compassionate

Night Gardener
Tends travelling souls
On astral missions
Into the silence of dreams
Moving through realms closed to most
Come a little closer
I cannot tell you more
Maybe soon
A glimmer of truth will flicker
Who knows

Time after time after time
Falling endlessly into incarnation
Always crying out
Am I anywhere near cooked yet
Tell me whose idea was this
Are you sure
It is not just a nasty joke

Rain soaked dreams
Spiral outward in the fading light
Past avenues of golden trees
There is more to come
Tomorrows sorrows lie in wait
Hiding in imaginary rooms

You are in transition
Your crazy drunkenness an allegory
Fall into another stupor
Swirl in your numbness
Do you remember anything
Be drunk again and again
Until you see
With closed eyes

Why are you dressed in plum red robes
I hear you ask
I have been sitting on this pole for years
Meditating watching and looking
And yes I have been through the eye of a needle
There is more to this existence
Than we can imagine

A generous compassion
Will soften your temper
Cease your anger
Move inward
Towards your centre
Go beyond sadness and grief
Look for clarity
Be compassionate

Night Gardener
Tends travelling souls
On astral missions
Into the silence of dreams
Moving through realms closed to most
Come a little closer
I cannot tell you more
Maybe soon
A glimmer of truth will flicker
Who knows

Time after time after time
Falling endlessly into incarnation
Always crying out
Am I anywhere near cooked yet
Tell me whose idea was this
Are you sure
It is not just a nasty joke

Rain soaked dreams
Spiral outward in the fading light
Past avenues of golden trees
There is more to come
Tomorrows sorrows lie in wait
Hiding in imaginary rooms

You are in transition
Your crazy drunkenness an allegory
Fall into another stupor
Swirl in your numbness
Do you remember anything
Be drunk again and again
Until you see
With closed eyes

In this unknown forest you
Stumble around like a drunkard
Looking for a moment of sanity
Chance is a clever thing
If we knew what it was
A door might open
Does anyone here know anything

Sensing each other
On this day with you
I sit here grateful
Being quiet together
In this pool of light
Fana is a joy more than words can say
A bliss beyond bliss

Stand alone
Wind and rain lash your face
Ice and snow tear your skin
Stand alone
Sun and heat bake you oven fresh
Owl teases your mind
You play with knowing and not knowing
Those two imposters
Dance around like whirlwinds
Seeking attention
Stand alone

A new perception appears
Eyes dart in all directions
Figures skulk in the shadows
Are you persuaded to look yet
The wounded doorbell rings again
I hear it but am too bleary eyed to move
We rush here there and everywhere
Hearing so many opinions
Trying to
Trying to
Trying to

Tell me what does this madness mean
This old healing house looks on
And gently breaths a sigh of relief

Golden flutes
Sweep away stagnant thoughts
Finally there is an opening
Lifetime after lifetime
I have longed for this moment
A fresh continent appears before my eyes
Time to move on
Time to migrate
Time to play exotic music

The Fusion Room doors open
Your invitation is waiting on the guest table
In the ocean there is no separation
All is entwined in oneness
Embrace it and become a Fusionista

Ravenous I sat at mountain-cloud gate
For eighteen years
And I did answer yes
But always the wrong yes
Is there a solution to this riddle
Desire rises and addicts get their fix
Emotional tsunamis give way
To a surreal pleasure
Body and language lay limp
Beached beaten and exhausted
And soul says
No solution
Try again try again

A desolate wind
Shouts our names as we sit here
In the desert night under the stars
Wrapping tongues around delicious understandings
That come from just knowing
Suddenly a harsh chill enters
And wearily we fall asleep on grey flag-stone floors
At first light a new tenderness arrives
And sweeps us clean

In the dark of the night
There is no moon reflection
Just tree leaves clapping time
Shaking and fluttering
Tree branches creaking and groaning
Dancing to ecstatic music
I came to taste your beauty
Turn your face eastwards
Wait patiently
The sun will raise again

Breaking out of this tavern for fools
How did I arrive
Who brought me here
Aeons must have passed
This wine is too intoxicating
My senses are dulled
And memory fried
I must sober-up and see with new eyes
Is there a way out of here
Can someone show me the door
I have to break out of this tavern for fools

Alone in Spain
On a warm road south
Watching a fresh new sunrise
Heart brimming over with
Passionate youthfulness
Expectations left behind
Everything before is gone
Only this sublime moment
Memory begins remembering
Anxiety splutters into life
Watch out for all those dangers
There is much more work to be done

Tears fall slowly down the window pane
A distance faint voice sings a lament
Snow pierces the lattice
Listen with heart and both ears
There are signs of inner movement
Move towards the one
Gather round the fire
And feel the joy of seeking

It is the system that is insane
You know it makes no sense
To engage with crazies
They only brings chaos
Sit quietly
Patiently
Waiting
Knowing
This insanity storm will pass
Inshallah

Walk away quickly
Do not look back
What was done is done
It is over gone finished
Remonstrating over legalities
Will only make matters worse
You asked what your crime was
We could not possibly tell you
But we do know
The trial will be long
Arduous and expensive

Street lights dimly glow
Stray cats stare into headlights
A donkey farts
A mushroom opens a door
Quiet out there I say
There are toads in here trying to sleep
Be careful where you step
Oh dear so much shit to avoid

Our intimacy is separated by the
Tick-tick-ticking of time
I long to reach across this divide
To embrace you
Yes but how dangerous is that embrace

Soon enough the lazy wind
Will become ferocious
Lashing out at everyone
No matter how guilty or innocent
Souls will be cleansed
With a sweeping passion
Are you ready to lose your beliefs
Because soon enough
You will

Today is a day unlike any other
I caught a glimpse of your work
A thousand footprints walking
Breaking branches falling
Raindrops dancing
To the beats of time

Obsession with time
In the dark forests
Of lies and deception
Limits imagination

Devotion comes at a price
Advice cannot be given here
As to the amount
But pay close attention
Wind is speaking with clarity

Standing in this city of souls
Seeing such homelessness
In a land of plenty
A spotlight shines
On your shame
On our shame
What have we become
Where has our kindness
Compassion and generosity gone

Your gentle kiss
Breathed a ray of hopefulness
Into this old form
My soul has been waiting for this
Now I am truly awakened
From this long dark slumber

Inside this solitude
I reached out
For a sliver of an answer
About infinity or anything
While in the garden
Rows of spring daffodils
Bow their heads
In silent prayers

The edge of the wind
Like a razor sharp knife
Cuts through fragmented emotions
Snipping tearing and scattering
We are rough stones
Being honed and polished
Into round shiny pebbles
Did you hear that
Listen
There it is again
Did you hear it
Does it sound familiar
There it is again
Where is it coming from
What is its source
Now I understand
It is coming from
You

A Child of the Land
Alone freezing and abandoned
Sitting in silence counting passing moments
Asking why has fate been so cruel
Suffering from a fear of fun
The notes of Hijaz sounding tell of a
Sadness beyond sadness
There are no more words

On this saddest of sad days soften your outrage
My lifelong friends and travelling companions
Fair Equitable and Just have gone into hiding
For a while until it is safe to be in public again
Greed Anger and Hatred have been unleashed
No longer restrained are strutting
And spitting venomous cruelties
Reason Moderation and Mediation have withdrawn
Leaving Callous Vicious and Cruel to run riot
Spreading their bile with impunity
But be patient with these monsters
When they have had their fill
With nothing left to devour
Fair Equitable and Just will return
Balance Calm and Tranquility
Will also reappear and join the party
Then the Sun will shine
And warm us once more

Buried deep inside
This outer sheath called self
Is the true me
Each day I wake
Itching to find that place
I look everywhere for clues
Being yourself is no easy task
Unlearning this inner corruption
Takes a lifetime perhaps more
I must trust that it will eventually appear

Drown in silence
Drown in misunderstanding
Drown in fullness
Welcome this drowning
As your drowning comes closer
Fall head first
Into the whole sea

Fanning the flames of fear
In this dusty village of beliefs
Those dark images loosen their hold
And are retreating into a dank cave
Forbidden to roam freely
Light is illuminating us now

In the Empty Quarter
Walking bare foot
Shifting sands
Stretch out over
Scorched horizons
Each fading footstep
Is a separate reality

We are witnesses
To an event so profound
And beyond imagination
That it is time to speak of
Love and hope for everyone
We came here for this
But are we ready

Too many words
Come spluttering
From the mouths
Of clever people with
Empty brains

Stop doubting
Open yourself
Lose that nagging voice
Policing your fears
Give yourself permission
To be true

Forget sermons and dogmas
Be like a Sufi
Be crazy
This life is a dance
Whirling turning and vibrating
Step off the blue train
End the chatter between
Dualism Materialism
Presentism and Eternalism
Go beyond yourself
And the gates of suffering

Walk the path of least resistance
Beyond hope and hopelessness
Beyond intellectualism and emotionalism
Beyond aspiration and liberation
Beyond wants and needs
Become an Adept
Oui Non or Puet-etre
You have begun the long walk home
No longer having to ask who am I
Gather yourself and walk beside me

Debt bondage makes us slaves
A new paradigm is emerging
Voices are screaming
We oppose deception
No Trumpanzees here
Institutionalised ridicule is terminated
Focus on the point of attention
Leave the programme
Matter is only energy frequency and vibration

Feeling refreshed
Like a Ney imbued
With sweet almond oil
New notes sound with
A fresh vitality
And a new purpose

Herds of thoughts like wild monkeys
Running in all directions
Poking tongues out
Making faces from the undergrowth
Corralling them to make even one coherent idea
Is like shouting at the moon

When I was young
I wanted to express everything
But had nothing of worth to say
Now I am old
A few words are enough
But my silence
Speaks much louder

Desert train dance
Hearts beating together
Feet moving in irregular time
To a sublime rhythm
Minds are drawn upwards
With over thinking
Clarity appears in rings of fire
Swallowed by monks
Chanting in glorious overtones

From here to there
Moving like a Bossa-Nova
Reality is on the blink
My vision has gone wonky
Seas are calm and the
Land gently ripples
The Mexican Penguin
Is asking for a ride home

Renounce worldly vanities
Wait for a revelation
Do not squander this precious
Gift of existence
Give sincere thanks
Show heartfelt kindness
And compassion to everything

Be alive to truth
Die to the Self
Lose possessions
That bind you
Refuse to be possessed

The Tower of Silence
Is where we go
To be scattered

The blue light of Sophia
Announced the arrival
Of an unexpected emissary
While I was negotiating
A peace treaty
With my
Self

What is the point of existence
Who started this pantomime
Of smoke mirrors and misdirection
Look for truth without form
Be what you can become
Leave that old head by the roadside
Stay still and alert
Move in the delight
Of knowing
That you do not know

Scream out loud
Scream out anger
Scream out pain
Scream out your power
Lose those ear demons
Whispering negativities
Scream out joyous expectations
Scream out beauty and love
Scream this from the hilltops
Scream from the inner depths
Scream long
Scream hard and
Scream loud

Stinks rising
From bullshit
Hits the nose
A fainting lotus
Opens

Dis ease of the mind
Fuels stagnant delusions
There is a cruel mockery
Drained of passion
Looking for connections
Put an end to these sorrows
Haul yourself out of the cesspit
Of helplessness
Be luminous
Hear that never ending note
Calling

Give yourself a chance to breathe
Nothing is so entrenched
That is cannot be moved to change
A cat only exerts enough energy
To fulfil its intention and purpose
Excess effort
Is a total waste of energy

Paul Cheneour has walked a broader musical path throughout his career embracing European Classical, Jazz, Arab, Indian, Celtic, and other music's, culminating in his own 'World Fusion' style.

"Tapping into the source of creativity takes great courage and even greater competence in acquired skills.
Paul Cheneour, a leading UK jazz, classical and ethnic flautist/composer suffered a near fatal car crash in '91.

He recovered with the conviction that he needed to use his talent, life, and near-death experience to explore a new form of creative expression. This amounts to an opening out to the influences available in the moment.

All the world's great musical and artistic traditions remain as resources and are no longer seen as restrictive boundaries"

(Interview extract by Michael Greevis for Colour Therapy Magazine UK. 1995)

www.ingramcontent.com/pod-product-compliance
Lightning Source LLC
Chambersburg PA
CBHW021135080526
44587CB00012B/1293